T0069013

TRIBUNAL

CRITICAL PROSE

The Grand Piano: An Experiment in Collective Autobiography (written with Rae
Armantrout, Steve Benson, Carla Harryman, Tom Mandel, Ted Pearson, Bob Perelman,
Kit Robinson, Ron Silliman, and Barrett Watten; Detroit: Mode A, 2006-10)

The Language of Inquiry (University of California Press, 2000)

Leningrad (written with Michael Davidson, Ron Silliman, Barrett Watten;
Mercury House, 1991)

VOLUMES OF POETRY TRANSLATED AND PUBLISHED IN OTHER LANGUAGES

Fatalisten (The Fatalist), tr. into Danish by Alexander Carnera
(Copenhagen: Det Poetiske Bureaus Forlag, 2018)

Pauza, rosa, chto-to na bumage (A Pause, a Rose, Something on Paper / My Life),
tr. into Russian by Ruslan Miranov (Moscow: Hosorog No. 7, 2018)

Ma Vie (My Life), tr. into French by Maïtreyi and Nicolas Pesquès
(Dijon, Presses du réel, 2016)

Gesualdo, tr. into Turkish by Uygar Asan (Kadikoy, Turkey: Nod, 2015)

Minha Vida (My Life), tr. into Portuguese by Mauricio Salles Vasconcelos
(Sao Paolo, Brazil: Dobra Editorial, 2014)

Felizmente (Happily), tr. into Spanish by Gidi Loza (Playas de Rosarito, Baja,
California: Editorial Piedra Cuervo, 2013)

Mi Vida (My Life), tr. into Spanish by Tatiana Lipkes
(Mexico City, Mexico: Mangos de Hacha, 2012)

from My Life, tr. into Japanese by Junichi Koizumi, Toshiro (Shige) Inoue,
Mamoru Mukaiyama, and Koichiro Yamauchi (Tokyo: Meltemia Press, 2012)

Mi Vida (My Life), tr. into Spanish by Pilar Vazquez and Esteban Pujals
(Tenerife, Spain: Acto Ediciones, 2011)

Gesualdo, tr. into French by Martin Richet (Marseilles: Jacataqua, 2009)

Lentement (Slowly), tr. into French by Virginie Poitrasson (Paris, 2006)

Mitt Liv (My Life and *My Life in the Nineties)*, tr. into Swedish by Niclas Nilsson
(Stockholm: Modernista, 2004)

Mit Liv (My Life), tr. into Danish by Jeppe Brixvold with Line Brandt
(Copenhagen: Borgen, 2001)

Jour de Chasse (The Hunt), tr. into French by Pierre Alferi
(Paris: Cahiers de Royaumont, 1992)

TRIBUNAL

Lyn Hejinian

OMNIDAWN PUBLISHING
OAKLAND, CALIFORNA
2019

Cover art:
Ostap Dragomoshchenko, *This Time We Are Both* (1985);
from the collection of the author; used with permission

Cover typeface: Trade Gothic LT Std
Interior typefaces: Adobe Garamond Pro, Hypatia Sans Pro
& Trade Gothic LT Std

Cover & interior design by Cassandra Smith

Printed in the United States
by Books International, Dulles, Virginia
On 55# Glatfelter B19 Antique
Acid Free Archival Quality Recycled Paper

Library of Congress Cataloging-in-Publication Data

Names: Hejinian, Lyn, author.
Title: Tribunal / Lyn Hejinian.
Description: Oakland, California : Omnidawn Publishing, 2019.
Identifiers: LCCN 2018040200 | ISBN 9781632430663 (pbk. : alk. paper)
Classification: LCC PS3558.E4735 A6 2019 | DDC 811/.54--dc23
LC record available at https://lccn.loc.gov/2018040200

Published by Omnidawn Publishing, Oakland, California
www.omnidawn.com (510) 237-5472   (800) 792-4957
10 9 8 7 6 5 4 3 2 1
ISBN: 978-1-63243-066-3

This book is dedicated gratefully
to
Hannah Ehrlinspiel and Taylor Johnston

with admiration and love

A Human of Mars

A HUMAN OF MARS

1

I am a human in the absence of others of a yet better red.

Omniscience is violent, infinite.

There are no straight lines except those I make, and I do this rarely.

I don't foresee that I'm here by choice or of necessity, perhaps I will never know or never want to know.

There are no birches here nor lemons nor elk nor signs of social insects, but there are flakes and something similar to red slate and mirages very close at hand.

2

I come from the Red Leaps—that's what I called the first new place and now am calling another.

Everything new comes at me and with me.

It is nothing but flame and all one flame or none and the same.

This world has a red edge, *that* might be lit by candlewicks, then cigarettes, headlights, blasts, and flares.

Red arts, red candies, red controls.

3

Even monosyllables are still rare in my conversations with myself, I have too little percussivity of thought.

Once I found webs that had formed between my fingers and toes and under my arms and between my legs—perhaps time once meant me to become airborne.

Let's begin then with that to which I might have fled, the original desiderata.

Red life that rises.

Red guitars, red occupations, red rills—it is midseason here and I need red skills.

4

Talkless the tongue looks—but I mean to say "lacks" or "likes," reveling (revealing) in the opening of my red mouth, pink gums, the release of salmon.

The grounds for my preoccupations here are iron rich.

The old coinage here is unready, leaden.

I cannot return trees to fire *in toto*.

This soil is the refuge of no previous profile and from that I must add my own and germinate new ones.

5

I am a tenant here of a rose.

Where, and what or who, is the ventriloquist?

Tone is yet to be learned, and I have yet to respond: mollified, or like a sculpted monument from rust risen from unlegislated sediment.

In silence ubiquitous I eat raspberries, binge on tomatoes, and dream of bleeding cows.

I am sucking red and scratching.

6

I am not *like* a soldier, nor *like* a beet—similitude here is inconsequential and best abandoned, as I am, yet to come.

War fever has yet to go elsewhere, with peace chasing after it, crossing a mile and then an ex-mile, but imprecisely.

There is no overcoming radish, lurching diphthong parachute, military cinema parcel, packaged snarl.

Time transits the bustling abyss.

Music isn't impossible when it's happening under the velocity of a solar shout, so gusts of xylophonic quaver have shifted my hair.

7

I don't live in comic melancholy, I'm choleric.

My mechanism is evolving from the ovulation of rubies, and my intellect generates rubrics.

Human of marvel, human of markets, human of marble, almost human here of eggy bones.

Of what use will be cock or cunt, they are cavernous, decorative, extrovert.

My brain is brick.

8

I somnambulate without moving a muscle, formed for freedomless forms.

Life is a paradox ergo three accuracies ergo levity, fear, and fate, or (waving Occam's razor) ergo ergo ergo.

Fetal admirals battle as commas claw, inklings of desperate sense.

Bound redbud trees and rosy yams and ironic russet clay.

I didn't lift a finger, or I did.

9

The past bounces to the future—or the present *is* that bounce.

I want to launch spectral red and do so and wherever it arrives it leaps into view.

It could be called foreground, or hot, or agricultural and vivid, or angry and amorous.

Lacking black, in red, as if without skin, the human of Mars can confess.

Wolf and woodpecker, throat and nut.

10

I must begin as a biographer of a paramecium, then be a biographer of an onion.

My day is 24 hours 39 minutes and some seconds long.

I don eyeglasses, yellow-tinted, and everywhere see citrus.

A comma brings me to a full brief stop, curling back it turns back, surveying the path surreptitiously, or preparing to put down a root.

Everything has a future but eventually not as itself.

11

There are no orgies here in solitude, no rosy orifices except of rock and dust.

All convexities are harsh as iron shields.

Some kind of love then—at all, so long.

Already I am membering.

From excrement I can extrapolate squalor and from that feral cats with which I'll co-exist and also peanut butter, robins, diesel fuel, and ticks.

12

I am almost removed.

Red prairie, red arithmetic, red reflection, red snow.

My dreams hold death in diamond drag.

Until I had a third person, I didn't know of my existence.

What does recent mean if not decrease of momentum.

13

Whose grass, whose permission, whose consciousness, whose urethra, scrotum, aorta, snatch will I discover and with what feet, fingers, teeth, tongue, nose, I ask, eyes closed.

Oyp, crinxk, dmout.

Should I list myself as once visible, then risible and audible and adaptable and capable and sexual and powerful and extreme?

The third person is consciousness, then come the red emotions and the second person appears.

The robin displays its Martian breast and martial stance—the robin: uprightest of birds.

14

A green human would be not complementary but abhorrent to a red human of Mars.

Red human now, pinning accumulation.

I could spit a pit.

Livid tongue.

On a green planet I come decamouflaged—visible predator and visible prey.

15

I'll emit a prying quiver, I'll be a spying given.

This is the work of a suspended thumb.

Data will accrue, as to a central consciousness that, in registering it, makes the case for it: rampant raspberry, bestraddled ruby-studded portico, drug-laced date-rape grape-bestrewn party punch.

Look—it's still: a lithoform tiger toiled from milk and mud, silk and crud.

There can never be too great a distance between subject and object nor one sufficiently small.

16

The human (so it was called and then subsequently culled) transmits: I'm here and all's clear.

I can live a year kissing and killing in delicate wickedness.

Homo bellicosus and belly-cursed.

Primal.

Whiling and circling no different sun.

17

I turn to wistful lingua, wit-filled languor, keeping the ode at my toe tips.

Red malice!

I'm not willing to exchange epistemology for religiosity nor phenomenology for ontology.

Perhaps I belong or have belonged to another "I"-space or many others.

A human will play for apple, muscle, and zipper, and all else she or he has a loose eye for.

18

Roseate palms and pink soles, crystalline spit, open nose—all predicating person—and there's more.

Witness my attempt to vermillion the misery of history and to bleed the history of mystery.

Alone and along again I'm as invisible as a fart, incontrovertible as a stinking fact in the air.

I've long lived the martial etcetera, eating cherries, tapping texts, sucking up and spinning straight, cop and cop out.

We will do it still: go for gold!

19

There is nothing that is pre-martial in the human.

I'll have Martian genitals.

Postulate: tiny speckled brown moth alighting suddenly on a page (or some other sweet small eventual randomly existential particular); counterproposal: irresolution; and another thing, yielding to a pause: a day in the life of a human of Mars.

Observing my ears, others (entering) will think I have come from snails.

Here's a torso, iron-rich and reddening.

20

Nyam, prit, olkralipous—none of these yet apply; spon, crankle, elroghtuiskess, writh, leat, mors—these must pertain to a different world.

I come to learn to use the orchestral rhetorics, gestures, smiles, to point, to shrug, to wave, to scowl, to beckon, nudge, poke, caress, to pommel, pinch, to knee, to tackle, to embrace, to punch.

I will propagate the concept of sparkling as well as that of burbling and firing.

I am a human of Martian origin straining to overween and overhear and understand and undergo and survive and surround and surrender to no one and then to everyone, that, a mere fiction: sheer universality, post-terrestrial, pre-alluvial, de facto, anomalous.

Werldwarrygnos, once immanent now imminent, is this, I think, and kiss a knee.

21

I delight in appearance.

What's over an egg—what's above it?

Priorities, proprieties, pieties: there's a pattern and into it humans of a certain kind thread themselves.

There are many days that have not yet been broken.

When I breed, as I must, I will have children—seventeen or thirty-four: Belinda-Fred, Gyorgy-Clarice, Nanos-Shereen, Mustafa-Pilar, Françoise-Mamadou, Lyuba-Claude, Pablo-Katrin, Teura-Yonatan, Jude-Anahit, Anita-Liam, Saida-Sam, Giuseppe-Hoa, Ping-Miguel, Isabella-Finn, Oleg-Aayusha, Salma-Gang, and the finest and most furious of them all Lou Cipher Lucy Fir.

22

I can see through the blindfold and I can't see through the blindfold—both of these statements are true.

Humanity is scattered in the details slung on the ready ruddy rust.

Go, says the painter to the poet: go, and stop progress!

Ghost of a red fruit, gaze of a red face, words on a red page.

Humanity is fated to break off, lose cypher, lump sum.

23

Joys are tiny things, my soul has a flat tip, the subject-object binarism is misleading and untrue.

Phenomena are oriole.

Red argues by chapter and verse, road agrees, copper goes green.

I am marooned in courage.

I have the opening mind of a vermillion infant splashing in an agony of water.

24

I rage like a mother when mold is on the salsa.

But the scarlet hill is plump, a subtle strategy, the horizon soft as belly fat.

Phenomena are woodpecker and cardinal and brought by goose.

Or, to put that another way: air is a medium for pathos and partnership: transterpretation, portation, transack.

There are interplanetary condiments—the stuff of space: salsas, true, but also relishes, jellies, mayonnaises, tapenades, mustards, marmalades, sauces, chutneys, ketchups, and jams.

25

I slurp, guzzle, dabble, delight: O dazzling geranium, silence on the purple pond!

I could crush this bug, exterminate its kind: I am the death in its life at the limits of visible light.

Yes: if you spread a red bed you'll pull pictures into your head.

An ode to exploiters and explorers from one of them yet to come begins above.

A foot is pressed in fellowship to the Martian crust.

26

I lack a blank mind.

Spheres of color hover on a deep plane; the red darts out.

Doubt is not coterminous with limitation; I am hot and bent with it, I am out with it.

Doubt is the Martian's demise.

I want to be without traditional consciousness, saturnine, lunatic, stellar.

27

A human puts spur to the moment and fingers to place.

Time is a series of unrelated sentences to be reread and then rewritten.

There is glue on the route.

Red goes to s/he who comes second.

Madly apparent, a human is perpetually in a phrase stage.

28

Wary, wearily, early—a human has two ears and purses them.

As a human I think to railroad my declarations with quandaries and queries.

O leisure, O lesion, O lesson.

It's said we'll have a filthy single purpose, half precisely, with toes and genitalia twinkling.

Always drink rose water with red meat, always spit the blood you could spill, never need nonsense but always allow it.

29

Life is a vehicle, carrying us around, hurtling us between plants, deploying us as living advertisements.

Us: we arrived and now have to sell everything we brought with us in order to leave.

Dear Reader and Readers and All Enlivened by Green Chlorophyll or Red Blood or Viscous Yellow or Ochre or Brown Fluid or Fluids or Fluidity or Blue, can I sell you my ankle or greatgrandmother or broom?

The rocks are down: petrifaction cannot hold.

Life is mother-father to troupes of entrepreneurs juggling bonds and sticks and bills and stocks and I'll eat them: a dish of scarlet olives.

30

Perhaps the insane fear they are incomprehensible and have a horror of not making sense, or perhaps they have a horror of doing so.

Posit ghost, posit flush plus flesh, then mates, neighbors, nations, then wars, or worship, oceans, anchors or acres or ankles on which dancers turn.

Some version of "I" is a cartoon pig, another a swiftness of a Naiad named Curl or populace failure.

Some time of myself is—what? certainly not a sentimental "not ever" or "when ever" or "back then."

♥!

31

Unspared self, softly, spoken, speaking.

Or do I only simulate dissent.

What is it that has consciousness, what is animate with perception, what experiences?

Pigs burrow, asphalt chokes, buildings arrogantly rise and crush.

That's what I am.

32

To part, parse, patch, and please.

Tales turn over many small things—tales turn over the pleasure of knowing.

Water falls.

It is a social truism that anything that is happening may become explanatory, may make history.

A stranded unleashed anchor lies at rest now in its funereal future, whisked under rust beside a massive gear shaft robbed of torque.

33

The multiple social classes, former and future, plus bumblebees coming through windows and plums enter imagination and occupy a temporary calm.

Dumb luck and drum bowls, thumb rhythms.

A red bedspread.

And now here is a thing with no clear utility, a thing without purpose, a thing just here, or it's meant as a perplexity, to perplex me, unless I can sell, trade, distribute, or share it.

Things for other things: the start of chronology.

34

O narcissism, collaboratively fulfilled!

O friendship!

O circular familiarity, which is, among other things (so many other things!) like an umbrella or mushroom or child's drawing of the blazing sun or like a marigold after rain or splattered egg yolk or an enormous chord in a minor key or like a human's chewing!

Living in a circle, moving around, escaping oneself, trying to forget the past, striving to remember the future.

Ludicrous chewing with lubricious malice between lewd jaws of lumpish meat in luminous light.

35

Lights begin to remove sound, name—therewith we have name-closure, nullity, the origination of sleep.

Time fingers fate, time fingers space.

War is bound to every moment like a bull to a boulder or a mote to a drop of dew.

At roar.

Humans are myths, at war with one another.

36

Arise, rice: I tend a rose: a rose and I.

Reality is composed, uncomposed, composed: no ant for itself, beetle through compost, king/queen on the heap: reality ahop.

Cherry trees without me and I without a kumquat tree.

Now other things must be acknowledged: a magnificent black mare, a crow of many trades, a white and orange kitten who knows all the songs and is a first class mimic, a peach, a flea, a good credit rating, the Google map app.

The riddle persists: who am I?

37

Things fall out, badly or well.

I depart, separating from myself and become a red image of it.

For a being like me—voluptuous but dainty, common as grass seed but unprepared, like one who reenters paradise and, finding it empty, seizes and fills it, feels it as hers or his since it is provisioning his or her febrile being, providing for his or her animal necessities—the future is an indispensable dimension.

But this is so far less than the more we can't even imagine that, as if I were solitary, "we" quakes.

Now for a library and then omniscience via wi-fi and sci-fi and street smarts, white wine, drought, handguns, dunk shots, hat tricks, STIs, size, sighs.

38

The head is a northern orphan without an itinerary.

Objects are a forethought.

Red fingers of white Martian, right pinky to right ear, left forefinger to right tit.

A general with his back out blushes at the frailty seen through field glasses: an inspector of Mars.

A chant goes up, a chart, of a human with arse.

39

Say that I am reproved for some reason—chastised—and I agree, I agree: that was awful, what I did, what I am; is this what it means to "have a bad conscience," and, if so, why do I have one?

The whole wing of the human hand, its feathers ruffled, is said to be a voiceless courier, striking a hard blow.

Bound where and by what, for what, to what?

Ash, driven into crevasses, notches, holes, stuck, chill, arcane: it has all but lost its struggle.

Rocks are bending, and the orb, remarkably red, is verging on black, as a dingo verges on dog, or male on female, ice on water, clout on charisma.

40

Disaster attracts; it roves, tempts, pulls at lives, draws whole societies into ruin, sucks from the vanishing points of being.

Continuity intercedes, the ceaseless breaks in.

A human loses itself in a harmful emotion framed by movements of air discernable in fluctuations of red.

Now Marta and Marshall, Marianna and Mary: they climb down. By "they" I mean "twice."

41

We desire grief—mourning without aftermath.

The quiet is air, the setting is sun; the red on which I rest is land and blood of some long past always passing into my presence.

We suffer disappointment, dismay, disaster: severed from placement and situation, severed from permissibility, severed from fate.

But what is this we?

Nothing repeats—nothing again.

42

There are many rules for multiple moods: pessimism or skepticism or cynicism or doubt with optimism or stubbornness or naiveté or sanguinity switches roles, and hence we have the naive skeptic, the cynical optimist, the sanguine doubter, and some of these are equine, some bovine, some canine, some ovine, some feline, some porcine, some caprine, and some are us, unbacked, awake, chanting "O language, o lexicon, let me sleep!"

Punctuation is plentiful.

Head an engine, body a ship—carrying what?: water, iron, viscera, calcium, adrenalin, bacteria, oxygen, urges, potassium, urine, blood, life—that kind of stuff as or along with ballast, fuel, machinery, and cargo, and a captain or capitano, capitanessa: a subject, an "I."

"I" now has a computer, an instrument for scanning, search, calculation, contact.

But there are still stars so there is still fate.

43

When the next hour or minute comes, how could anyone recognize it as the future?

The future arrives bearing something futuristic—a new kind of battery, a substitute for the sun.

That magnificent star-strewn vault, under which we dreamed last night and that seemed to promise us a beautiful day today, hasn't kept its word.

True; but what if the fog, which is hovering above the ground, collapses from the sheer weight of the moisture it's carrying?

Humans fall out, have a falling out.

44

A planet comes whole, home to a system, but can it carry details that disobey the system?

A stream of elements, of turbulence, of petulance, of elephants.

An elephant can't float like a cloud over a savannah, but—there!—we have pictured one doing so: have we defied the system?

Indifference loses us, and all that advances chases after the sun.

From the spheres comes music and with it a lyric: "Now a pause, now a rose, and now a small coffin, Bitch!"

45

What hollows us so profoundly that we have an interior into which we can descend?

The future comes, seeking knowledge with its limbs, ears, and eye holes, to which minutiae respond and are deemed an explanation while the human mourns its loss of magnitude, its lack of anything entire.

Let's say the past arrives: a row of horses, doors, each one of which or whom is a soldier: a militant of Mars.

There ensues baffled slaughter spread on water, patterned individuals, variables of time.

What if, on the other hand, it drifts over a desert and rises into the upper atmosphere where, as a chemist might put it, it dehydrates—dry slaughter, aridity untimed?

46

Surreptitious, sub rosa, underground, but not unphenomenal; segmented, rich in chemoreceptors, hermaphroditic: such is a marsworm.

A planetary pulse—a pause, and then we resume our relentless living.

A flicker in the present of a discontinuous sunrise.

What will I do if I wait and see, what kind of pause would that be?

Lacking memory, one would be unable to perceive motion, unable in time to see what's real.

47

Waves of saying, waves of seeing.

Well ray and frost rag and battle: we have ourselves an ethnic Martian.

Circle power turns, circle panic serves: a social circle, a city circle: blast drawn blood purr, story lock, malediction, work: work in a narcotized drift, in owlish exchange.

Description, which always includes an element of retrospection, is nonetheless forward looking: more blood purpose.

From far away drifts the sound of a white small adorable yapping fluffy defiant curious ownerless male dog—abandoned, castrated, feral, fawning, he howls in the dark at Mars.

48

What is disappointment if not awareness that a joy one has received is being taken back.

Culinary parsing, red parsimony, panned parsley.

If I were very great, I'd command furrow, old proverbs, and red bread.

Already I know how to swallow spinach and how to rise from the ground, dusting the rust from my butt after the long lust of a waking sleep.

Already triumphantly I feel I am living on an exalted plane, as, seeing the vast trees blown by the wind, boughs leaping, trunks swaying, I recognize the power and am exultant: exalted by exultance, or exalted by consciousness of my capacity for exultance.

49

I am a teacher of Mars, advocating math and pathos.

The despicable, delicate, cyclical damp.

Always or.

Lament, rage, and hilarity: manifestations of loss of control.

Straining agonistic genitals, and all the rest: is *this* "morality"?

50

And yet I'm a juvenile giant—somewhat vulpine, though also concubine, visibly pinkish-raced and bipedal and inedible—my bellicosity only in this context suppressed—and, like this one, I'll fill the next stubborn moment that occurs with animation.

Nations excel at vengeance, the sexual and financial and racial and architectural pounce and possession.

But every particular that has endured its history has earned its theory.

The runnels barely undulate, the range suffers semantic delay.

I drift, drag, draw: red mouth behind green lips, gnawing wilted minutes.

51

This is that primary world, red.

I can't get a grip on it, my similes don't stick, its crimson has no period.

I yearn for green peas, since it is with green peas that I might most subtly learn the tactics of revenge.

I have no snout.

I am incarnadined; the world is washed on me.

52

I had no plans to come; I never knew I had gone.

There was only one, so it was general: milkmaid of Mars, plumber of Mars, academician of Mars, mayor of Mars, secretary of Mars, Martian chef and sous-chef and dishwasher, mechanic of Mars, its poet, mathematician, historian, army, shopkeeper, and housewife.

Pleasure without leisure—a human of Mars is an orifice.

If there were things to name, I'd apply Sparrow-Wide, Vise-Anvil, Wire-Arrow, Mars-Crow, Angle, and I could go on, my naming capacities are endless.

The world is an oyster and I am a Valentine.

Afterword

I sought to express with red and green the terrible human passions.

VINCENT VAN GOGH

And you, red judge, if you were to tell out loud all that you have already done in thought, everyone would cry, "Away with this filth and this poisonous worm."

FRIEDRICH NIETZSCHE

TIME OF TYRANNY

TIME OF TYRANNY

1

Anxiety, ambition, energy, and sleep are caretaking
fish in the deep black sea, my sweet, the black deep sea. Yes
and I tossed a twig
the x, y, z of unrest and loss of privilege
they never had, the vanquished Inca
at the sharp angle of a perfect rainbow and afterwards Jupiter appeared
of which the Rocky Mountains are like mules hauling oats
perceived by senses, words, a set of names
in music. All this should scare the legislators
noble and real and we are crazy and smell smoke
for entertainment, social bonding, and great anxiety,
that trinity of apricot, scalp musk, and gas
of life where light first falls on the passenger
who is briny and upright, but like a dwindling cornflower.

2

I'm not too old to dance meadowlarks: great punctuation
locks in black and blocks, crepuscular and vain the sun
in its descent. Throwing hats we kicked up dust
of which the Ural Mountains are but dim reminders
through a wooded alley loud as if disturbed
in the unbuttoned fog that grays a pedestrian's silhouette
while the passport picture reaching out to me is true or false
to tetrahedral nation-states dead in winter water, enzyme ice.
I cannot fear to be forgotten, a child
born, another book, the dust at dusk
of skilled blind sculptors whose cities sink
the swollen toad, flung foot in the air, and boy
flowers, flamingoes, flames the red tips of prophetic pride
singeing history, its grand punctuation.

3

Language is a victim of its own success
while into the carriage comes a louder lyric me
of which the Cockscomb Mountains are like apples rotting in the dust
that none of us would be content to leave unlifted
from a caterpillar's cud to chew. Placebo's pills
can kill, pour planks, and call. People are forced
to live, work, yearn with bourgeois linearity to change
this rake-wielding life upon row upon row upon row
of the river pulled further and further away
under the unswallowed elegy of a collared stork.
Then productivity as reproductivity ends. Motion
gets immobilized by perception into things perceptions get
but perception gets it wrong from quantum habits
of sadness, the scent of a wet sack, granite fumes.

4

Doing is highly thought of and frequently abandoned
as at a bus stop beside a stunted gingko, and time
is tossed, a laundry pile large as the crown of a tree
or the gravid animal of Pythagoras, and every mathematician dies
while runnels vacillate or do nothing astrophysically speaking.
Let's go for eggs and to the bakery. My kid wants to be
a puppeteer. But someone must polish glass and since then the refugees
weep wax and travel over agate pastures and gag.
But we have to trust philosophy and deny the property
where depiction most perfectly depiction depicts.
In a faux chateau of finance the proposition is a picture
of corn cakes, last crumbs, weapons passing from hand to hand.
Let's rest. Life is fast. As the city rat, resuming, says: "Rudeness
is rude." But what kind of ego would utter that?

5

Runts have their tools and outlive lust and age
with introspection rewritten one word at a time of
humility with notes descending. Music goes to hell
to cruise that heavenly neighborhood with a strong wing,
the horse a ruby roan. Patterns of judgment, chess
of text, respect that cannot sleep as night falls on the shores
before an infant knows of time that there is something
in mathematics shorn of ideology. The public
does not need to be convinced. An idiom
like Kierkegaard on Halloween gathering twigs
and fathering eggs while a stunted thorn
frolics in the shade now dead inconsistently down the large white sea
does what a poem does, making itself
understood, industriously caging a tune.

6

Every situation can be taken as subject to a proposition
at stake at this stage of the state. Rejection of a context
need not be of one's own hoeing
of the sun, one's head a building site. Say I rode in on a vicious mule
surrounded by leaves under the northern star, the eternal conflict.
Say I beat my brow and only put on shows, withered
webs, a rigmarole, an atrocity to which I'll give no words. refuse it
representation. The janitor is innocent, autumn is ill, and cruelty
will be the rule until I die from a flea bite or while beating
a metal drum, eating honey and corn like a girl again
with an umbrella under a redwood tree with all of which I am
in a certain sense one. The roof on trust of hover can't render love
pathetic. I claim too much and yield to the Bighorn Mountains
of which the truth of history is but an indifferent silence.

7

Because we refuse to personify the gaping east or deformed west
or cranial north or sacrificial south we must accept this box
and these panoramas to which we were led through sliding doors
just as certain Alpine cliffs reproduce the "head" variants of Mayan "script"
with an impersonal cluck from a jeweler, merchant of knives.
Wherever a human is to be found, there you will find
occupation, a skyscraper, a 9-foot copper weathervane, imperial pickles,
a force plundering an unarmed ceramic bowl.
Urban greenbelts lift a feisty allegorical vegetation in human voice
above an opium fish, a dime in cinders under the wind
and there are wealthy men, skin not yet charred. They are popular
as hardware, music, poached eggs, immodesty, multicolored snapdragons
and the alphabet sacrificed in times of need. I live under the authority
of a stucco beehive, which is a weighty cinematic mound.

8

We think, we approach, we exist
sweep and speak, on ziplines or not.
Sayings spread as amusements for children women and men
by pony-poets, beetle-poets, crow-poets
are voiced by the words themselves and not by anyone speaking them.
I dab fingernail polish on six croquet balls. Which
of the names of Hercules do you hear and in which of your ways
of which the hill behind the soldier bathed in sweat is like a general's nose
or the yellow bowl upturned beside the kitchen sink
to dry. It's now a wedding finch a reference to whistling
rain, a great honesty in the far sacerdotal south.
They piss on the spider, the aged face
of the great organizer on slender evidence, the rising
sun that hangs a grass fed puppet from its hands.

9

The mountaineer rappels at midnight the wall a wall
the wall a woman recalls: a contingent object, it might never have existed
then you look at your fists and there are the letters o
in admonition, odor, foot. A dog shakes premonitions
from its coat, lovers of time—time of all kinds—
winged insects, mosquitoes mostly but also moths.
Welcome, unwelcome, buffeted, who can make durable wax,
who can knot? The baker is a man and brutalizes wheat
and all attempts recall a textual residue of celebrating rats
a game of backgammon with dancing kissing getting drunk
hugging singing crying when we were leaving war
a stumbling block reconstructed and constructed
o xank history thistle etspung hatchet right
or wrong, corvid head over human heels, facing insurrection.

10

Pity combatants on the line who self-concretize, becoming paving stones
but I say too loudly that of which I don't know how to say enough
borrowing transcription from a local pebble held in a palm
from which a puppet tugs as if pulled by the revolutions of the planets
Mercury Saturn or Mars over nearly twelve and a half million days
marking time, which is the subject matter of history
in which the sun itself bakes the bread then drawn from the oven
and cooling under the proprietary nakedness of the caustic trees.
So, asked a bee of experience, how is it that umbrellas are raised
against the future of the sun? Remnants of the past
don't expect us, remnants of the past didn't foretell us.
Our songs are sonically shattered over shortwave by a scop
singing the praises of his patron, the racist acquitted—he nods
and mongers the derelict pattern, a never vanishing world.

11

People work under the clouds and are direct
inheritors of the things that happen every twenty days.
What saddle do we use? A wolf has been caught
and it sweats. Such allegories do not unfold in easy procession
which is called lustrous, erect, major, and will in some field cease
altogether. Tyranny narrows, faking solicitude.
The chains obey, the dogs piss under glass, voracious
fish leap from the beams, we do arbitrary things—appear
and disappear as leonine as flies. The first person
is made for oneself, denizen of a cult or rubbish heap
ready for the evening show in the cavern of centuries. The second
is made for you, a respectable human of greenish hue.
We had a drink and it cost a house
into which we moved, music coming like aphorisms from stone.

12

Drift of grief a feather that scarcely seems to fall
or feature. Future a chair standing on a counter with Cuisinart
quietly in its nest. We sniff our underarms and sing at intervals
and nail captions onto facades, we are like corn kernels clapping
on their cob under the eyes of the neo fascists who have always been
among us, ascending bougainvillea vines onto roofs
up decaffeinated trees in the dark. Tyranny scuttles forth
harbinger of vertigo. Under the stars there are many things
with capacity to collide or combine with other things
in our vicinity (that gravitational field of monsters). Tyranny's gropings
are cruel, tortures sociable. Do they stop
there, the sun brown and female, illicit, sulphuric, and fucked
but conceiving such joy as that which leaps from phrases
like "made of quiet beans" and "music the dunes."

13

Words hang from his tongue which he has bitten
saying "territorial terrarium" because it is a joke he says,
"wolf" to alleviate the tongue pain. Names make him
walk between dots on circles shoveled
in a corner where desire has deliquesced
into very windy surly foulness newly built
with deviant speech and sins of the tongue
and of the impoverished poplars, American beside my coffee,
an army major at once in an eternal army
stationed on a perennial battlefield for an undying cause
whose every combatant in her or his monotony
is pumped from a boom box
hot, exotic, and able to do something *really* well
and be a presence in the present tense of the foreordained.

14

The name of which the name pops sorrowfully and labor-filled
from the 365 days of the true year, the first, would be of something
in white shoes sipping lemonade and dead in her tracks
and there would be budding dust, small flies: they'd totter: female
and female relatives dodging bees
in orbit, captions composed by tyrants extolling tyranny
of broad appeal to individualists always arrogant, always
afraid of which the Appalachian mountains are only inconclusive
tales. Palomino centaurs more horse than human become geraniums
of church under clotheslines monumental now in their failure,
it's all too linear and I thought the popinjay
some kind of bird injustice speaks assertively
of its identity—or claim to identifiability—of blame
the tyrants were too drunk to remember and couldn't name.

15

A charity-performing puppeteer with laurel branch leaves
curves mid-air, unholstering his or her unconcealed carry grille
on which to barbecue reflecting meadowlarks seized
from the arid breeze as militants, each foot unfortunate
but handsome, kind, entire, and tired approach the city. Imagine:
panting horses and the pull, the push of heated time. They graze
on blowing hay after a run over grammar surpassing livelihood
under excelling oak or laurel, madrone, past pepper trees, sword ferns,
and a gnat laughing at each great beast's despair at something small
of which the Ural Mountains breathing salt are but history's disdain
for the dormant and the dead. A puppet cannot discipline
the emotional responses of those who are sent away and hack
through brambles; they are Babylonian or Antipodean or formerly Soviet
or Nazi or like a poodle, performers of a tragedy in a circus wittily uncurled.

16

The foreman of the regimental puppet show
hissed at me and I could only hang my head
a gray stone encircled by a band of white sedimentary
stone signaling yes, that's it, stone
signaling a day, the first
of a future year mathematically proven
by latching calcium onto a congruent cog over a 52-year period
of war awaiting critique waged by the week, hour, minute
we force to act, we force to micturate, we force to gadgetize
instantiate, frame, monetize, grade
the chord which is to take us into a dangling room
so that rain flow will not flaw
the road along which orchards order shadows claiming distance
controlled by the familial near and domestic dear. I stop.

17

Faces are long streaks emphasizing repetitive bonds
but temporal round destinations—all endpoints—make
no sense. I am bound unequal to a screen, the task
and show a drone dove grey in nervy clutches going
back and forth from one house to the next front over the leafblowers, o
the leafblowers: they monitor the orange colors of the solar system
and its textures and its magistrates overseeing poverty
or make that property doing its shedding of blood red shells
and shields and, too, sine qua non par excellence the pantry shelf
is better versed in math of which the Atlas Mountains
are like the mythological remains of the darker dead corpus
of humanity that (though logical) was strange. Round as space
and character but not as fate is the first date on the unbroken calendar
of the mouthed language, contralto, and weakening.

18

The days of the seven almonds have passed out of the public sphere
of a great number of trees beside the Sacramento River
of which the San Gabriel Mountains are to the sun
what a scrap of orange peel is to beauty
which with its glossy green leaves produces poultices
applied—or unapplied?—somewhere down an alley, short
and morally blind. How could we know which
if any is a radiant number with lucky energy? It's not mere chance
that the kids on the dance floor are boys and girls with M27 IARs
and great and guileless national price with which peace of mind
is incompatible. Time is ingenious, impatient, dueling. The dull
of heart go and come, the sharp arrive in black slashed with obsidian
blades. They have now fallen and dry in the dirt
over the money soldiers are served by their mothers, conspicuous life.

19

Where resisting. When cloud. How a ring tone, a bone, a well. Some
he or she rings a bell, he or she dies and receives an athlete's eulogy
and is an orangutan with unrehearsed high spirits seeking
no revenge despite high wind in the morning
and unnatural trees, hair lank in the afternoon is white
and orange and has descended from the clouds to go.
How there. It was then that the astrologer tripped over
gossamer. Then began the reign of an energized rabbit. Why
a numerical system combatting with the sun at the end of a tilted long number
and behind a blue and red and orange and green and white tile
like another end of the world, whose origins are unknown? A fish
and not its fin when bird, how wing, with moonlight
to waver water which is why we never went away
again against a stormy sky. With wayside. Where forbearance.

20

Do we crash conversing or confessing each thought, every idea, all
feelings of distant bulletins queasily liberated? Do we pick up
a bundle of witching sticks, do we loop hope, do we digitally display
our private things to public thugs in a white wood cabinet of billionaires?
I do not know, sister, cousin, colonel, mother. Some of us are undertaking
a task too late in the past of the future of the pine tree of excitement
one very warm morning which was very warm but overcast, the clouds
the color of tea as it flows over the deteriorating lower waterfall
of the Blue Ridge Mountains of which hot weather is but a mirage
representing gently the rhythms of comparison. Logic can rot
a stovepipe. What is a stovepipe, brother, nurse, granny, father?
Will we die drowsily? My cat is a troop of violinists, my heart
is a flame of rain dripping down a tree into a pond, the water level
incident by incident educated. Why does anyone want finesse or less?

21

Reflected glow nosing through the underpass. A lame eternal trucker fed
on buttermilk biscuits and oil disappears, so self-effacing as to have become
anonymous, so self-critical as to have become ominous. Sweet
is the tuck of the chardonnay the word for kitchen, fish, ringtone,
glitch of which the Khyber Pass is but a site
for whispering as one passes *whence, whither,* and *hitherto.* You will
make rapid progress, I hope, like wind over clay, gray
pavement, a new car around a new tyrant to whom the cock replies
nothing I am willing to understand, he is a frightened frightener
and fear is greater than daring, greater than divinity, greater
than a russet fox in a warehouse. Real estate can become
a woolen coat around a mannequin beset by moths afloat
in fame, a curly coat. No wonder winged folk complain. Sickness
is a social thing and language is a medium for passing news.

22

How lengthy the arbitrary seems and how often it returns
in the form of a puppy's snout or as a flounder's face. The arbitrary
can vary its head and make no sense by scribbling
with pen on paper in a microsecond just as a gardener can
uproot a paralytic azalea and plant pliant bamboo in the cuff
of a shelf with a lamp on it behind a screen. Boom! Is it a joke,
a coffee house, on a soldier's mother, o murderers? For that
which is not conscious, conditions are unstable, miniscule,
mobile, mixed, and producing microtones inaudible to the human
ear, an object of terrible neglect. Argumentative voices rise
above a cloud out of nowhere like an aurora borealis
of the colonial era of which we are the heiresses and heirs
and heavies hiding behind regret, self-denigration, quivering
eyelids over many odd events and an idea of the rest.

23

Dear in my head the free skull saying dread
almost melted my heat of impatient disappointment
which like a honeysuckle around a sycamore has wrinkled
already the oncoming epic timber adventure of which seers
saw to foresee but in solitude and without insults borne
by news and views mongered with all kinds of candor and untrue
benevolence a cat the color of a wicker wastebasket or peanut
on which to gorge. Certainties collapse, uncertainties
proliferate, and what is it really to punctuate further
like this: the mouse. The mouse a kiss, the kiss
a resistant clerk. Fold it. Headlines have got a lot to say
and almost always with puppets dangling from the hands
of waiters with wary eyes half-open half-closed over brown
stains. The animal head dog is a mere moment of rust.

24

Now note the slinking thirsty cat. We were forced out
of the twentieth century through some curious history, smoke
pigeon blue in a spirit of irony not on a beast's
birthday, ferocious boar or meandering stag
beetle or brute philandering flirt to be fathomed
by love of death and description. Declarative sentences
are descriptive often but are rarely simultaneous
with what they describe. We describe a resounding alarm
that terrifies the vulnerable of the perfect psychological system
known as profit pattern and sonic static and nuts and bolts
of thunder penetrating mass to enter cup as liquid
gallantry funds and wines, death under the sign of dirty fingernails
not of things but of the unfortunate gulf between ideals
totally contaminated which means the sun of which there are many.

25

A forehead stone, a cop's right hand, and inert ideology unbeknownst
are in a marriage plot of the new west. The old folks seem to vibrate
pictures at a slim young giant at a gate
and we become a group of which the Kunlun Mountains
are but a chain of taverns full of deeds in needy repetition
but of whose needs? The Mayan calendar is round and accurate
only within a range of 52 years, a table under a tree in a neighborhood
of mourning historians. What we cannot disinaugurate we must consider
worthless, cynical, despotic, dangerous, and too heavily deranged. Rain
of days, spoilage, suppers of battered sandwiches carried one step
further and then another we must let do their worst while we occupy
a place beside a western offspring under a dry conifer
where we retie into anarchic bonds the shimmering cobblestones
of an open university where, *par exemple*, we learn of an open universe.

26

On this day of this year of tyranny when the freeways have been
taken everywhere by you all so the erotic still not so much shy
as improbable can shine like a chord of many scales
into the dark at such high speed that we can see the dark
of all that's done and glare while growing older. Death seems to be
staying on its side so as to pursue its course and copy
life, a pillar in the morning of our subsequent love and the same
at night. Not so long gone are the days of the bachelor and lynching
cowboys as they return in the grey twilight just as we reach
home from a concert tour entailing many sacrifices
through seven American cities afraid our souls are measured
like time bundling days. Microtyrannies reduce constellations
repeatedly, reduce and reorder, while ravens craving air and shining
eggplants disappear into like landscapes in an expanding coastal fog.

27

In the emerging emergency some drink and dance and this is short
parity individuating an assembly burning in some taboo sequence
aboard a train bearing bodies and there you are. Are you still working
hard? Yes. I'm grizzled and plodding
as before I cried in vain my name, my rage. Glass
benefits us all and so do eggs and legs and disguise. Who are you?
I'm dance shovel gust, prompting long disdain. So what? I'm not
loneliness replying, blasting. On one side and another of "the future"
realization of what is actually happening "now" must come
before we forget why it matters and our faces
are under shrouds. We dream and shout. We shout more
angrily and awaken sadness. Fear is…. No, it's not
like an invasion of moths into winter wools. Fear is incomparable.
It is the innards of awful things and their engine.

28

Small creeks, very hot. Saw prison written and published
as the repository of unassimilable education, early history,
at which my heart aspired and my heart
fluttered, was refuted, and failed. I am a rocking horse, a cow
and yes always a goose upon a fetid golden egg under a vine
up which Jack climbs, purveying macho havoc, becoming
bird over mud under airplanes and a cloud, nubile
as tyranny, the sky introduced to electric light. High
and plummeting and avoiding swerve, eschewing
accident defying portent and the balding of the old
who feel unfollowed and unfated. No more sword, Uzi up
on eBay, prowess surrendered to pimps who market it
with demands for strict self-examination and pomp
plump as swollen legs in stockings. Noxious humid wind.

29

Dishonest happiness— of which the White Mountains are
but giant frogs as winter approaches shrinking
their throat skin and sinking into mud. Thus begins the erasure
and we are drinking eternally to and fro like a one dollar bill
unable to find a dollar's worth of milk in the bustle
of social life by cornfields, a fair, we've earned it by selling the cans
we put our compost in. Nails come through
the professional grade fireworks plate glass screen showing another
singer and new scenery conjuring from zero times
any number of plumbing earthworms, disturbed birches, serpentine
floodplains with mosquitoes up to as many as thirteen
wigglers in the pale relativity of the water glass on the window
sill in a fated place. True divisions—things that divide and make
divisions true of them—are producing happiness. False information.

30

An irrational flux crosses a mirror image and original
mutual disdain drawn blank. Cowgirls, o cowboys, we are out
of control. Ungovernable let's be at the top
of a hollow tree. It won't say no but its position
is of beauty proper difficult and problematic as a world
in which you (?) close the walls and leave
forever and call the past "sweet times" but "treacherous"
and "expensive" but "twisting around" and "womanly"
which doesn't block neatly. Ornamental scrawls, week-like
but not week-long, include and that's a system of unarmed annotation
with which on the legs of dull scissors to pursue sense
held up to starlight over the Caucasus Mountains for which heaven
is no refuge and without comparison and empty of cattle
for rambling cowboys who are gilded and only for show.

31

Tyranny asks in simple question form to what and where
the infant refers when she speaks first
words before vanity fatally knows remorse as a fist, a fox
in a vineyard chaos to which grapes are tied or bound
subservient and gendered as breasts, bosoms, boobs
eternal. The fox in the revolutionary plot dies in the leafage
in its feeble conquest of the exhausted voices breast-feeding
thoughts made a spectacle, a crime, a viewing
by police, time thieves, and media, and the weeping guiltless
very much in black down too naming amorphous russet pools
at the door dammed to stagnate. Pathos unfettered
and anarchic as umber fleas or ungovernable hallucinations waits
to see when everything will turn out and why and won't
maintain abstinence after the fact that can't be rationalized.

32

And history an enemy of things, a queen
with her long eyes, degenerate brain, and massive ovaries
incarcerated with a ball, a cone, a tragedy of progeny to inflict
through prison sugar on what but a fine evening carefully hewn
from the emptily particular ordeal, the never final blow
from the stick of a drummer in a battered band. Attention: anarchy!
And its assistant: poetry!—of which the Mississippi River
rises as a woman deprived of sex by her ninth child
loved unwanted at her breast, her heavy chest. Similarities
are like a rope, a kind of thirst: identity! identity! This
and there: that's an animate being arriving like a hornet over a patty
buzzing of ground beef, its indeliberate dance, a sequence of signs
in brilliant ecstasies of history: which lake, that cloud,
perfected effects of the slow life of a quickening fight.

33

Once the elevator—it's about the descent of grease, the gloss a lowering
of self-esteem, the redirection of a woman's consciousness to a wish
in being dead to die to be dying to fight back
to back with her self-consciousness held in high and rising esteem
on quiet claws under the stripes of a tiger or trumpeting synonym
for the ferocity of mothers in their kindness to others
in merriment pouncing and catching rice in steam rising
from pots simmering over the fires of time. And then the milk
from consequential heads—note the bulging eye and the tooth
an enchanting curl which beckons like a nautilus shell
fallen on a false facade. Is love yet queen? The horizon with its undulations
crawls. Then other questions arise: why can't I sleep? It is well known
the elevator rises and falls and is inured to each vigorous season
and is not borne down by misery nor raised by the joy of revolt.

34

Pathos, patience, kindness without fear of death: metonymy, it is
a sail, contingent, ambiguous, and tense, while civil
conversation no longer prevails without dark repair
to violence. Structures swell, embrace without erotic intent
the discrepancy between dollars earned and soapy whispers
in the ear. Time alone is hateful and at face value
vague. An egg. It carries a heavy load, apple composing
zebra. At sea the word goes down in humiliation, like kindness
pixelated back and digital. Wealth comes in microwaves
and it can saturate what we say, but I mean only to describe averted heads
no longer signaling the will to hear nor even swear obedience
to belief. The suns set. A car goes by. The costs are myriad
for those who are as myriad as the hours it will take
kindly to decide how to make changes and what they should be.

35

So much for the trees, rather than careful, and the hateful
weeping of the street sleeper's machine it seems
with entrails turning and returning a place
to sweep like the stinking edge of a dog in the long hard stare
of moonlight upon a scintillating form to be filled out. Analogies
spread, one spawning the next and then disappearing
into ambient time, the moans of context, the loss
of the game: goal reached prematurely, before the victim
is bagged. So! So very tall and continuous is the skin above all
to an egg laid in Guatemala by a precisely mottled hen of browns
unmuted. What a shell! How subtly slow anarchy might shatter the windows
that lock out the great cycle of streets with their fleshy jaws
jutting cheeks, rather than shameful, and the logical
day of the night laborer or someone like an arborist or dermatologist.

36

Cruelty in increments with measured equanimity is given through
the back and broken windows of voting goners flocking
their own enunciating greatness and the return to a bloody barn
from the bottom of the sea in its inconsequentiality
sloshing the ordinary times over those who flee or drown
and did not even rock the cruelty of separation, departure,
disappearance. My neighbor is a resourceful woman
whose curling fang got milked. She heard false taps of attention
at the inglorious white dairy doors. Ignore the echoes, dimples
networked and broadcast as significant. Call the cows, repaint
the floors of which the River Thames is but ceaseless turbulence
no better than a name. It can be changed, rebranded, layered, and turned
into prose of a gas generator. The power is out and this is just a dull
apocalypse on an ordinary day with typical loss.

37

One day to wake to a nation's national nationalism indebted
to orange, lighting one from the day to mistake green ash
and the mountain indistinct beyond the River Ganges
of which the outcome must remain unthought
as dissolution is to the body of some old artist wielding zinc
white. Mists of incomprehension farted by a clown—an initiative
and the Mayans scowl 400 years before and hence. The nurses
told me and the musicians and all the coffee shop staff: don't start yet
where I'm stopping for a bit and I wish you all
an excellent recovery and may we soon have victory
for those who will arrive right here despite bad shoes, false
steps that press like the seal of a tyrant on a death
sentence sneered, sentence snorted, snort snotted
into an unnatural tissue. I press the unrhymed palm to my head.

38

And then without disadvantage one Thursday night without
falsehood to dream without authority to judge or to lie
of things too odd to suckle that flare under feasting vultures
by the sea: mere local violence, though near. Next
there is a nameless eggshell or a broken mushroom
prospering in the char checked shirt of storm
from which cold refugees wave global devotion being
born among us biting battlements with bitter faith. But I won't bore
you with the exclusive showing of my dreams to me
from which, not wanting to participate, I leave.
No. That's dreamt too particularly during a bout
of insomnia producing global delusions of freedom. Next
there is an open door that dreaming softens then obliterates,
its bulging eye sealing the gridded lips uncomforted by sex.

39

That friend now liberated from the tyranny of our lexicon
and the era of the Inuit and Wintu still to come
stands between the toes of compromise. There have to be animals
inhabiting the weasel state with loss of blood
so great are the tyrannies of skitterbugs and skin. Pride
is an impediment toward which one word
can lead larger than life higher than the Adirondacks
of which a haunting image is but another word
for snow shrinking under varied lighting at its description.
Lost. The dotting of the face, a curl, decimation
of a population, and fleshless lower jaw the date: zero
a grotesque bird, a turkey vulture chasing the sun
as it northward sets into my eyes its tyranny of light
leaving history with courage in its severed hands.

40

Time: a saddening effect affecting limbs and great androgynies
of papier-mâché. I shouldn't willfully get angry at the space
around it blindsided in a light unfavorable to it by wasps
over meat. You should see it all converting, or so they say. Hay
an artist admired in its stacks harboring rats grew under an arm
pit or over genitals of a grandmother or as the streaming tail
of a horse on parade under a malnourished marionette. No one
would feed its lack of subtlety: time and the puppet, they gallop
to war where they become smaller and smaller, like grapefruits
bisected and the size of yellow split peas before which people
crouch. They are self-down-grading. Their anxieties descend
with content on and all around them. They are people but who
knows who or what they've done with their miraculous fat bones
pierced by numbered silver rings as from a bell.

41

In a season like lute music for a drone and our fingers
plunge, the winding rain is wet on the pages of a *Pacific Coast
Handbook of Trees* the property of populist survivalists mingling
with the mist under which the Santa Cruz Mountains are but childhoods
whose tops line fragrant passageways for flight as trembling, lulled,
whiled away, and interminable as anthropomorphosis
and misleading comparisons. Until now. Something has been my life
and I will not let it be taken from me. I will not go mad
by being greed mad, money mad, fame mad, hungering, lusting, even
loving. What? I am excited by mistrust. I am put
off. Some have used poeisis to shape a private safe
zone entirely their own. Is this mass incarceration of clowns?
Let black bloc anarchists and reflecting stars break the bars
monumentally cast into stolen rock faces masked by "deictic trash."

42

What are a paradox's chances of survival and how
might we apply them, you a truthful human
or a synonym avoiding exposure? Small are the apples, fallen
the peaches, bruised the yellow lopsided pears, diverging,
divagating, bifurcating, split, part face. For life in a creek, a god
of wood must be buoyant—that profane, that frog. The political
is sick, the striving creeks are dry under a rheumatic empty
spout. Things a stringer might string are missing. They are
gone like money and family photos and identity and cards
from a wallet poorly formatted, very small and looming large
as disconnected salt from glass, tears, and a mind
controlling a spectacle. The light is a loose unit, a slack streak
of something through but without shadow entirely
now apart from the usual specimen of anguish and word in English.

43

We build a likely seat on which to hunker
bodily day and tunneling night over toast like a blank screen
we have forgotten. Chicanery is our progenitor. We complain
about blank complications, we espouse fur-bearing passions. Mister Rat
welcomes this with immersive glee and we become late and dead
as certainty. We perpetrate and dread demagoguery as we dread
the rat but we love dissent as we love to make deviled eggs
for our forty-eight children and left, left, left, right, left
to the red-hued mall to buy sauerkraut (refresh), ground
beef (refresh), vodka and a hoe, a welding torch and tank, a first aid kit
and a gift card which I will hope to receive as suddenly as it comes
to me. I confess my faults because I am sure we will all be seen
as the turning heads in the impenitent landscape. The redwood trees
through all weather spiting inattention leap like an alphabet into space.

44

Skin and social class are accidents of birth—sort of
like while unlike shallows in the Nile River
whose depths are in the air of human aspiration and will
and confession prolonged by Ingmar Bergman's *Wild Strawberries*
during a storm in March soon perishing and wept away
in blotches on a great taut toil. Animals and dainty flowers, authors
and recipients of soil—may they peacefully travail
throughout a restless night tossing in that bed
those fingers clasping dark air's dream craving's fear
of tyrannical bedding's bank, border, and bridging. Grazing
light lights upon destruction and disordering of mileage, milieu, the resistance
of the unannounced medium: ink or milk. Taking a day
under tyranny of earth upon the whole pretty well
the thundering mountains of which the names resound are dappled.

45

Here full-length and all untenable in what beginning with date
and place of death the profiles report are longhaul semis
under camouflage and command where horses would misbehave.
Badly the bullions win, the beetle is plucked, the mother
is a broody figure rounding round her legs both drought
and sun's disdain for intimidation and the obsolescence of fun
to be had between hands and legs of which the Concord River
is but a confession given in contradiction to any
actual memories. Meanwhile the mountains
are ready-mades and ten hours early while later
than the hands modeling liquid dwellings for clay
refugees. They are as original as childhood
and each day on a calendar has a sign and must be signed
to ascribe as death what's invincible and improvised.

46

Cruelty advances and guns over dogs. They fall
behind crocodiles vicious under blankets behind
binoculars, they give competition to the fiery captive
Lamborghini. The genie in the everyday is the closing
signless measure spanning the de facto rumor drawn
from the real with dotted scars from the voracious war that eats
the evening of patriotic fun with primeval paternal finesse.
But how much farther can we go I cannot fairly
watch or say. Ghosts have lost their fur and all narrative
sense, have not arrived to reverse history, order
meaning. Logic is but a serenading trio proclaiming maternal sorrow
and the permanence of departure, the difficulty
of retreat, the otherness of the escape
at which dogs cock their ears, sharp as shells.

47

Delusions come true under a deep dark sky, my dear, over
a hill that my head ached in the morning to spin
otherwise than as it spins or has been spun like a dark room
with wealth in a bowl heavy with handguns dredged from the Rio
Grande and Orinoco and Zambezi Rivers compared
to which relations between nations are like flows
without freedom. Tension dislodges shoelaces protocols
pebbles and hope-autocthonous rodents
driven from cultivated fields as derived bodies of positions
of knowledge: a fob activating an intelligent car: brand name
Nietzsche. What will transit wickedly is a given day
to which withering wind or grass returns like an apple
to its core coerced. We will use dimension and negotiation
of maternal love and thereby inaugurate the trivial: quotidian joy.

48

People love that so and so performs *I can kill
the monster mildly* apologizing as I am
a monster So-and-So and stand, stake, snail as one
of the founding volunteers at a doorway leading into a small void in the whole
world which is all its own just as the words such people resist are all as loud
as my feet for themselves are free. No shovel, no jackhammer, no
stirrups, no horse, no truck. From all shores humans in all weathers shed tears
which we uncertain in our times find irrecuparable and surround
with doubts, watching for the monster. It is all awful
or exciting. In our arrogance we humans remonstrate and mount. It's all legal
as is polarization and loss of time and the cutting off of lip and preservation
of the tongue with which to beg for absolution and water
from the River Guden which shudders on its way as if inspired
by medieval songs composed in the years of the plague.

49

We live in toppled times under a feat of tyranny; let's not
fake getting lost, let's do it, let's not do it intermittently, let's be
lost, disoriented and never to be bound so all can hear
the hiss of the adverbs we shoot into tyrants' eyes, quivering
shafts slippery from limbs and aimed by eyes under feathered
lids. Our features are like stale bread, my headache bad
as a blueprint for butter. Windows: how stupidly the intensity
of glass returns to us the terror of love. Things diverge, separate
like the forks of the Eel River to which the competing lies
of two tyrants are but split stones shaken by earthquakes
of stupefying times, of minutes through a glorious forest, of women
who are personal friends, the flanks of a prevented rabbit: to scatter
and ambiguate, obviate, surreptitiously
flesh and hurry to find things to recombine.

50

Birds hatch, eggs are laid, nests are built, trees branch, seeds
sprout: it's always time. Time to recognize the sipping
self as girded shelf supporting stuff conducive to supporting self
recognizing time making its attempt to install
itself with all its belongings. They include forebodings
and long descriptions of the rifle butts that press
against the past shouldered by the men of firing squads
and the verminous skin of dogs with mange even at a very young
age outside cafes or on short chains as if their existence
were a prerequisite to mastering the arts of being
delicately human and a gambler with a passion for mortality
and substituting one value (vivacity) for another (history)
upon the heads of humans grotesque as the programs
they invent to send their opinions forward.

51

To discover time, to become conscious that the present is
and does change the air as a pebble can't between
the crenellations of a castle in the captured air, is to crash
into one's self. It's fantastic, a fantasy with a fandom fanning
a fan in the form of a hand splayed to move the foul air
of timelessness. Wandering in waves is the fate of personality
which, like the octopus, is as smart as me but with less
shape than the foothills of Mount Etna once seen across a bay
on which the ships of tyranny went from left to right
to impose tedium, an interesting phenomenon, foundational
to feeling. It won't be wasted. Haste is a scourge but a very small
implement, speeding is a needle incapable of penetrating
time, which is carved in great detail into ephemera, which linger
with patience and are inevitable and inevitably strong.

52

Together we all devalued the tyranny of value
of which the Monashee Mountains are but peaks perched on a single branch
of a boundary marking pine tree, a stack of inches, a time
frame within which the anxieties of the young are like pigeons ashamed
before a goose beset by wizening luck and love. Weird
as cabbage is reminiscence, interpretation donkeys, intersections
revolve, we play cards and glitter with skepticism which we find
better than a scythe, it *is* the present directed at our patience. Elusive chords
drip, milk generates its own reward of which the plumage
of any egret is a mere suggestion and muslin a mockery
which tyranny cannot thaw, torture cannot make
unkind. On a white bird drawn by chance words are what
but a trundling shock, come too near, then setting off
in attendant sparks that ignite a conflagration of opinion.

Afterword

The world seized and whirled me.
W.E.B. Du Bois

There is and there can be no poetics which prevents the living experience of countless perceiving subjects from being killed and buried in art objects. So, does this mean that art objects ("works") are products of the alienation of our culture, whose other finished products are produced for self-annihilation?
Christa Wolf

Ring Burial

Ring Burial

1

A work of art is a prophetic loan, drawn on fugitive premises; the artist acts on it, and, presumably, sustains some faith that others will do so too, or at least could.

For the present, timing is everything.

Overhead a configuration of crows appears.

Times slide.

Predictions are a different matter; a massive earthquake is coming, as is the death of the sun, tyranny, another wedding, more war.

The trees rise, elm against fascism, ash against misogyny, unalienated beech, free willow, trees presenting continuous oak.

It is only by *silencing* the dead that Death can resist them.

2

Fate, dividing and matching, is the energizer.

A circle of bling on the finger, the finger up in flames.

A system of discrepancies, dissonances, near misses, precarious matches.

3

What is the social event for which this is intended?

Two rays of the sun, tongue and tongue.

Writers and readers share a home-taking urge: home-making, ring-bearing.

4

How does one escape oneself if not by also escaping time (and that I would refuse to do on [socio-political] principle).

5

Autobiographies reflect Romanticism's residue.

6

Bearing crows good will, I assume it is reciprocated.

But good will can change—it is mostly just an act of interpretation.

Every word is for something; it must be because of this that writings are acts of desire.

7

Do we experience the logical per se (affecting us, say, with satisfaction), or do we experience merely a sequence of occurrences or set of things, of which being in a logical relationship is only one of their constituting elements?

Life being what it is, it is more than what it seems to be.

A first purchaser purchases a tree, the next a chocolate turtle in a jar.

An hour later, when folding a towel, the second purchaser is feeling both satisfaction and distress, she mutters "paragraph beak."

Rubble is the quintessential allegorical material, the stuff of future meanings.

Out of laughter, astonishment spreads, bewilders, demolishes.

Now the body is freed from the obligation to generate a story.

8

An *unreasonable* Apollo: a wild sun.

It is easier to form phrases than to state senses.

One could apply one's emotions (best or worst) or the pathetic remains of one's convictions to almost any situation; one could be guided by resentment or by compassion; one could be drawn across the street by the plangent playing of a violinist busking in the sunlight; one could refuse as a cynic to be drawn by anything at all.

To live half naked beside the sea is a recognizable fiction that proceeds through events such as fucking on the beach or the grating of a hull on Grecian sand white as the snow through which a suicidal mountaineer trudges to his or her willed affirmative death which is nothing other than a contribution to breaths of air drawn by elephants.

Yet none of this contented us while all of it did which is true of cantaloupes dimpled but round and of a saintly nature, eschewing leaders, inured to inimical critics, rotting in due course, or eaten.

9

Unpacked, unprocessed, but bereaved—I have cut into the bark, removed and rustled it, like a cowboy with heifers calved from my head and now on the loose pursued by vigilantes.

A sense of frustration grows—who wrote that?

Whose hand carried out the attack, the theft?

Who was (or is) sad?

And at what location did the event or events occur?

And what was the size of the human population in the world at the time—or what is it now—in China, in California?

Congestion—fertility is great and exercised early; people are ubiquitous, becoming a population; there isn't enough water; the climate reacts, contracts, redacts.

10

Unable to distinguish between what I have wanted and what others wanted from me, I either developed or devolved into she from whom others wanted things, my importance not my own, and then I no longer had what anyone wanted and that importance fell away.

11

The tyrant closes the world tightly around himself, he is in the embrace of his own narcissism.

With the melancholy of self-condemnation and a pen, I, also a tyrant, draw a wall.

Stand, attend, account, shout.

All ideas but no acts so no association, no activism, no theater.

A tyrant proclaims that the future dreams of him, which only means that old age dreams of him.

12

The gradual and not necessarily melancholy deactivation of will continues, concomitant with sensitivity to the myriad activities of ongoing, random, impervious, and largely unredirectable life.

Walking the city streets, moving toward deanimation,

Does one disintegrate or rigidify in response to the anxiety of living?

Books or cds or perhaps inexpensive objets d'art and mementos proliferate in rooms or are cleared away, tossed or "gifted."

There's no such thing as knowing what you are going to say and no such thing as having said it.

13

The raspberries couldn't possibly survive the three day journey from the field where I picked them to those to whom I sent them: as a gift? as an insult?

Allegorical fruit, fabled raspberries: they could serve as points of reference (reference rotting, or more abstractly referential rot).

Energy reversed, the arrow is shot from the wound.

14

The birds fly, crows at white supremacists, sparrows at thieving corporate executives, just mallards at negligent landlords, free wrens at racist cops, pigeons contributing continuity, robins providing ribald joy.

15

A throw of laundry is made under a cold sky of gleaming ivory light.

From somewhere nearby a woman's voice shouts: "Go away, we don't like crows!" but I feel otherwise, having trust in them.

Imagine an essay in which the terms *temporal communities* and *semantic blizzards* occur.

16

Genitalia are sometimes peripheral circles, shadows, or, like the Pleiades, assemblages in the dark.

A couple is kissing in the shadow of a building at the edge of the plaza, the statement briefer than a description, her hand at the back of his neck, his right knee slightly bent.

The inferior party must steer, below a whisper, clear.

17

Beings push, cross; they encounter; they buzz, reproduce, quiver as they horrify and invent.

Being is a leaning note, becoming until absolutely everything has become.

When entropy is complete, differentiation is done, all difference is gone; homogeneity is ubiquitous, total, stable, pale; there's nothing but incest, and then a single vowel—no gabble, no swells.

Note: spring is mostly for animal tracks, and for trackers—hunters—invigorated by the activity of stalking, which is built into the very concept of romantic love, something from which the buried have fled.

Or, rather, something from which the dead only seem to have fled—perhaps in vain, perhaps tethered.

18

The future defies timing
Spaces gather.

Predilections repeat, accrue, laying down sediments, depositing life that's been lived, living that is gone.

19

Anything that is unlimited must also be undetermined.

This does not mean that it is unnecessitated, however, nor that it will be uncaused.

It only means that it is inevitable but that we don't know what the causes will be, nor even *what* will cause *them*.

20

How does one come apart?

Over the course of some years, one achieves—or, at least, attains—survival.

Adventures, coincidence, decisions, mishaps, risk, and luck are involved.

Fun is had, sadness is endured.

Rice is steamed, embraces are exchanged, boots purchased, shirts washed, floors swept, and bargains made.

And then disvival begins.

I come face to face with a still life, but it isn't even *still*; even *it* isn't still.

21

There has been a great removal of women from history.

Sometimes the women have taken the children with them, into the parlor or deep into the forest between trees.

Each on her two strong legs, women support a commodious space under their skirts.

They worship the first thing they notice in the morning for the day, they worship the last thing they remember of the day for the night.

Circularity puts the lie to progress, progress is belied by history, history eventuates return.

22

It's irrational to take the prophetic seriously, doing so is generally characteristic of the credulous or superstitious or blindly faithful.

23

Say that color is the language with which the sun speaks to humans on earth, or that color is the syntax of the language of light.

Color makes evident the push and pull of light in time.

Closure rejects and exhibits its rejection.

24

Is the statement "This matters!" a deception?

Why, then, does beauty bring disquiet?

My body is whole but incomplete, intact but effluent.

Property: it's that with which one identifies or is identified, one's metonyms.

It has brought about a sob, shaken from me by the lateness of the sunlit trees.

25

Soul loss leads to dizziness, then contradictory opinions, moods incompatible with one's actions, erratic behavior.

Efforts to track and retrieve lost souls fail.

Trembling under a new head of state, the body politic is falling apart.

Dogs fall silent, cats attack trees.

Protestors clog stairways, block freeways.

26

What if I say "I've been born into the wrong time, in the wrong place, into the wrong species" or "I've chosen the wrong friends, wrong family, wrong profession, wrong house, clothes, curtains, cats, toothbrush, politics"?

I do not doubt that some great writers have turned poeisis into a means of creating for themselves a private safe zone.

Take Hamlet, who has the time to live because he does not act.

Take Bonnard, who lets the wall paper absorb the presence of cats or women in the room.

Raging is at the ready, but unresolved.

Along come number and garbage, years and pus/spit/snot/ sweat/ menstrual blood/shit—and babies.

All get cast into the years of piss and possibility or impossibility.

27

   Sunday, Thursday, the 6th perhaps, or the 25th, no matter—what
can "vast" possibly mean, or "important," or "yours," when applied to
things that are familiar, or given, or at hand?
   Birds—they carry out a formal commitment, as do reptiles, fish,
gastropods, bacteria—a set of obligations.
   Life is fringed, frayed, tattered, worn, beclouded, buried, we miss
the point, we blunt it, and ultimately entropy dulls it.

28

   The entropic swallows, swells—subsumes, devours, folds.

29

   Some say the soul is a mechanism for processing impressions,
acquiring impressions, producing thoughts.
   Or water-borne idiocies, crepuscular rag rugs, fungus rings in a
forest.
   Out of memories we spin our sense of "identity" but out of
forgetting, too.
   Strong impression of blind windows on a blank wall.
   Sunlight is molecular, imbricated in the material chaos and the
radiance emanating from things.
   Phrases speed.
   Under foot, under the nasturtiums, underestimated (overlooked?)
earthworms burrow, copulate—or whatever.

30

   Force enlists form to assist it in producing a stupendous, an
astonishing, an orbiting body.

31

Faintly in the background, a luting hen is clucking over her lucid egg, her looming egg, her lurid egg, and who would disagree, who would complain?

Who are *you*?

We are almost equal, aren't we?

Pfft: we are gone, right?

This is the point at which the writing ceases, right?

Later a sentence, like a spinning drill but digging, buries a sense of the turn of a term.

And you—you should not be marginalized, you should not be cursed out.

32

A work of art incurs a debt, owed to history and the times that carry it; the artist can never pay it, but, presumably, assumes that others will do so, or at least could.

Each history throws its loop unit onto the ground or incomprehensible crystals in the wind circling the pole.

Not like a greyhound on a track, I think, but like a cheetah on the equator.

Enlightened resourcefulness becomes predatory, tyrannical in the frantic sense, like a dog on a leash leaping at a conifer.

There's a twinge in the shin of the tree.

Emotions have grown flaccid (in part due to the ever-increasing number of them), love is lax, and the optical nerves (like all nerves) are torpid.

Tyrannized, consciousness orbits the world, vexed, exacerbating bodies to which it's all the while obliged.

33

Sincerity is a form of clarity, clarity is antithetical to candor, candor makes a grab for attention.

But each of these belongs to a disorderly temporality—the temporality of the unpredictable.

Does sleep separate body from mind, so as to release the latter for dreaming, and pause the fire, dramatize the cardboard box?

34

Anti-determinative, interminable, incomplete—the poem has nothing to do with truth or value.

This poem, for example, is philosophical, in that it doesn't seek things to believe but things not to believe.

Every sentence records a stretch of becoming invented as it goes.

It's decontextualization, rather than discontinuation, that time effects.

Both time and decontextualization may generate obscurity but so too might structure, otherness, and particularity even more than entropy.

35

A bowl of thimbles, a chapter on ubiquity—and why not?

The toxic shadows history.

A fugitive gesture is made by fleeing lovers dashing past—a "fabulous performance motivated by nothing" with nothing in pursuit and nothing ahead.

A painter draws her brush across a corner of a canvas, making the last line of the painting.

The slopes whistle.

36

Superfluous sentences appear, but theoretically there is no such thing as superfluity; reality is everchanging but never spills out of reality.

Then what isn't reality?

Superfluity?

Is decay, deteriorization, dying, a means of eliminating superfluity?

Great waves are allegorized as cupbearers, but they can be best translated as immersive.

Reality is long since begun, like an improvisation but precisely unlike it.

The process continues, and, if one looks, one can find signs of it anywhere: in dirt under a fingernail, across the slashed skin of a snare drum, in the yellow-green residue left by a squashed bug.

37

Chance breaks off, a sputtering motor continuing time.
Reality goes faster than a rabbit in a meadow.
The soul must go faster than an ambulance chaser, faster than email.

38

From some eventual vantage point all this will be seen as just a mess of misleading clues, inaccessibly the stuff of life.

And yet, though it's true that none of us will be able to appear, all of us will have done so.

Each through her own two strong eyes, some women watch the fish swimming through the rustling leaves of the linden tree.

To lessen their regret at growing old, they minimize suspense, rising with the coming day clearly in mind, but left with unsaid thoughts and unthought things to say.

What possible event or object do we imagine when we call something "open to interpretation" and why is its status diminished by being so called?

Fiction and reality are involved, reciprocally determined, reciprocally undetermining.

Different things on the same road no longer part of the last life they were living are now passing a clump of wild iris as they enter a park, but the park is like an elderly human.

39

At times it will seem that I'm being attacked by a snake, at others that I am one.

Then I will remember myself, but I don't know whether this will cause me astonishment or fear or amusement or embarrassment or something I can't yet imagine.

What is the solitary moment into which this is extended?

40

Survivors are aggravated effects (of war, drought, and myriad other catastrophes).

Their survival brings about their poverty; few survive.

But, by definition, survival is something without time limit, so all survive.

41

The mind is subject to magnetic variation—but whose mind, which minds.

The smell of rain on the pavement evokes sensations, then emotions very close to memories but without content: splashes darkening concrete.

Bereft and encircled, orbiting and walking: there is a poet: a found child, an autodidact, eating a peach; here is a lone cowboy riding into a valley looking for work.

Memories link us to our world as does fantasy.

Capacities—a taste for raspberries, preference for cobalt blue, pulsating love—flung by the humble sea squirt.

42

The deep tomorrow is still just a tepid stone, still damp as a parked car's windshield in the fog.

Time extends the limits of reality, just as reality extends the limits of time.

Like a geochemist planning the past, some immortal, voice inaudible, must be waiting for her thoughts to slow or her heart to stop.

43

Many things are inadmissible but they enter anyway, like turds into a swimming pool, or acne on a face.

Time never just rests like a luxuriant streak above the earth.

In admiration of phenomena without purpose, I turned on the engine of the unaspiring car.

44

Fluorescent overcoat, nullified chest—are these narrative choices, salient details, identifying features of a tragic character?

45

Images are pulled, like thumbtacks from a wall—removing identity, to which we want to be invisible.

46

Fate went out the window, thrown by oblivioned hands into stirring dust.

Fate is radial—time's entrance into space.

The lines of a poem descend, but must it be into lyric obscurity?

What about lines bound by, and binding one to, household chores, small drawings, and metaphors?

Looking down from the edge of a pit, one might (but almost certainly wouldn't) see a russet panther pacing the pit's circumference.

47

I hardly sleep—in the solitude of excitement.
I feel betrayed, even by my own abilities and turns of mind.
Endlessness for many—but for *us*?
And the limping pigeon—how might it have injured its limb?
Arriving at an emotion we conclude an argument.
A grief system.
Time (history) withdraws tradition, takes up its own itinerary.

48

On a hillock in the grasslands—some 50 million years ago—moist spasms of occasional thought occurred, a girlish prank was played, and a hominid shuddered from an incipient feeling history.

49

The female is not an idle thing lying amid other instruments of labor, quite the contrary, she wields them, she wields them with her will, they are her body parts and broom, hammer, scythe, spatula, pencil, spit, and word.

The male adds a child to the household, in time the child shouts, exhilarated by the moving walkway whose direction she counters by running in a direction of her own, for now she knows no antagonist.

Policies are spread—across bedding, into beers, over sand—and tugged from salaries, salience—but they have deeper roots than these.

50

Mass incarceration is a manifestation of massive social negligence; "society" puts people in prison in order to further its neglect of them.

Let's imagine that we can read all the works of Henry James as studies in the limits of freedom (Ezra Pound long ago suggested we do so).

What is the pathos of art but recognition of this?

Must it be the unalluring task of the human consciousness, bloated and belly-up, to forget so as be free of vengefulness and regret?

Consciousness is discontinuous, just as a photograph is, grabbed from continuity and sent seeking a moment without time and without end.

51

Demise is mere background and irrelevant.

Love shimmers a narrative of leaving reality on oil songs behind.

Matter is a matter of self-betrayal without an ability to confess.

To revolt is to inquire, to continue as undead.

Can entropy improvise?

52

Turns of mind have woven a web—a fence—confining rabbits, elk, alpacas, and millions of square kilometers and those who, seen from above, move about flailing under a cloud of dust.

Narratives fold.

If they didn't, there would be no intensity at all, nor any obscurity, interstices, hiding places and refuges, anonymity, cunts, brains.

To atomism, the senses can contribute little, and not only because atoms as such are unknown to the senses

Extinction has turned out to be something to play with, humans in hats engaged in annihilation reducing what there is to perceive, diminishing what might appear before people who love appearances, animal heads on puppets that dangle from strings now eternally.

53

Descent! Submersion!

The actual world—see the children march into it! the girls twirl across its threshold! the men sweep it! the women cook for it (or cook it)!

The critical ring is in danger when the critique is tamed.

Afterword

Ruins give us a shock of vanishing materiality. Suddenly our critical lens changes, and instead of marveling at grand projects and utopian designs, we begin to notice weeds and dandelions in the crevices of the stones, cracks on modern transparencies [...].

SVETLANA BOYM

Regardless of whatever creation, work of art, or deed has come about, someone has lived. Are we someone? Are you someone? Try to be someone!

JULIA KRISTEVA

A Human of Mars

Sections 1-7, 9-15, 52, in slightly different versions, were published in Douglas Messerli, ed., *The Pip Anthology of World Poetry of the 21ˢᵗ Century*, volume 10; online spring 2017 at http://greeninteger.com/pdfs/010-poetry-anthology.pdf.

The quotations comprising the "Afterword" are, respectively, from: Vincent van Gogh, *Corréspondénce general*, number 533 (letter dated 1888), cited in John Gage, *Practice and Meaning from Antiquity to Abstraction*; Friedrich Nietzsche, *Thus Spoke Zarathustra*; Walter Kaufman, tr. (NY: Viking Compass Edition, 1966), 38.

Time of Tyranny

1-10: in slightly different versions published in online journal *The Spectacle*, issue 3 (January 2017); thespectacle.wustl.edu.

1-18: in slightly different versions published in James Byrne and Robert Sheppard, eds., *Atlantic Drift: An Anthology of Poetry and Poetics* (Ormskirk, UK: Edgehill University Press, 2017)1: *for entertainment, social bonding, and great anxiety* is a phrase taken from Emily V. Thornbury, *Becoming a Poet in Anglo-Saxon England* (Cambridge, UK: Cambridge University Press, 2014), 6.

1: published as a broadside to coincide with a reading at the Pulitzer Arts Foundation, St. Louis, February, 2017.

2: published on the Poetry Project website.

3, 7, 8, 10, 12, 19: published in *Hambone*, 2017.

13: *with deviant speech and sins of the tongue* is adapted from a comment made by Spencer Strub, PhD student in the UC Berkeley English Department, September 22, 2016.

31: for the second line (*with her long eyes, degenerate brain, and massive ovaries*) see James L. Gould & Carol Grant Gould, *Animal Architects: Building and the Evolution of Intelligence* (NY: Basic Books, 2007), 121.

34: *contingent, ambiguous, and tense* is derived from Sharon Hecker, "Life, Work, and Era," in *Medardo Rosso: Experiments in Light and Form* (St. Louis: Pulitzer Arts Foundation, 2017), 20.

civil conversation no longer prevails is a rephrasing of a remark by Colleen Lye in response to the polarization of thought manifest on the University of California, Berkeley campus in 2016 and 2017. Her original remark was "Civil conversation is no longer possible," which she intended as descriptive of a state of affairs that renders people dedicated to civil discourse powerless.

41: *deictic trash*: my thanks to Eric Falci for the term.

The quotations that comprise the "Afterword" are from: Christa Wolf, *Patterns of Childhood*, Ursule Molinaro and Hedwig Rappolt trans. (NY: Farrar, Straus and Giroux, 1980), 119; W.E.B. Du Bois, *The Autobiography of W. E. Burghardt Du Bois*, (1968), 195.

RING BURIAL

26: *Take Hamlet, who has the time to live because he does not act*: Jacques Rancière, *Aisthesis: Scenes from the Aesthetic Regime of Art*; Zakir Paul, trans. (London & NY: Verso, 2013), 118. Rancière is quoting Mallarmé.

Take Bonnard, who lets the wall paper absorb the presence of cats or women in the room: ibid, 119.

35: *fabulous performance motivated by nothing*: Jacques Rancière, *Aisthesis: Scenes from the Aesthetic Regime of Art*, 82.

46: *oblivioned hands*: See Diana Thow's translation of "La Libellula"/"The Dragonfly," in Amelia Roselli, *Hospital Series* (Los Angeles: Otis Books, 2017), 33.

The "Afterword" quotations are from: Svetlana Boym, "Ruinophilia: Appreciation of Ruins," accessed 2/13/2017 online at monumenttotransformation.org/.../ruinophilia/ruinophilia-appreciation-of-ruins-svetla... as adapted from Svetlana Boym, *Architecture of The Off-Modern* (NY: Architectural Press, 2008); Julia Kristeva, *Hannah Arendt* (NY: Columbia Univ. Press, 2001), xi.

photo by: Jacki Ochs

Lyn Hejinian teaches at the University of California, Berkeley, where her academic work is addressed principally to modernist, postmodern, and contemporary poetry and poetics, with a particular interest in avant-garde movements and the social practices they entail. She is the author of over twenty volumes of poetry and critical prose. With Barrett Watten, she is the co-editor of *A Guide to Poetics Journal: Writing in the Expanded Field 1982-1998*, and the related *Poetics Journal Digital Archive* (Wesleyan University Press, 2013/2015). She is the co-director (with Travis Ortiz) of *Atelos*, a literary project commissioning and publishing cross-genre work by poets, and the co-editor (with Jane Gregory and Claire Marie Stancek) of Nion Editions, a chapbook press. In addition to her other academic work, she has in recent years been involved in anti-privatization activism at the University of California, Berkeley.

Tribunal
by Lyn Hejinian

Cover art:
Ostap Dragomoshchenko, *This Time We Are Both* (1985);
from the collection of the author; used with permission

Cover typeface: Trade Gothic LT Std
Interior typefaces: Adobe Garamond Pro, Hypatia Sans Pro
& Trade Gothic LT Std

Cover & interior design by Cassandra Smith

Printed in the United States
by Books International, Dulles, Virginia
On 55# Glatfelter B19 Antique
Acid Free Archival Quality Recycled Paper

Publication of this book was made possible in part by gifts from:
Mary Mackey
Francesca Bell
Katherine & John Gravendyk, in honor of Hillary Gravendyk
The New Place Fund

Omnidawn Publishing
Oakland, California
Staff and Volunteers, 2018–2019
Rusty Morrison & Ken Keegan, senior editors & co-publishers
Gillian Olivia Blythe Hamel, senior poetry editor & editor, *OmniVerse*
Trisha Peck, managing editor & program director
Cassandra Smith, poetry editor & book designer
Sharon Zetter, poetry editor and book designer
Liza Flum, poetry editor
Avren Keating, poetry editor & fiction editor
Juliana Paslay, fiction editor
Gail Aronson, fiction editor
SD Sumner, copyeditor
Emily Alexander, marketing manager
Lucy Burns, marketing assistant
Anna Morrison, marketing and editorial assistant
Terry A. Taplin, marketing assistant, social media
Caeden Dudley, editorial production assistant
Hiba Mohammadi, marketing assistant